Cover photo: Civilians under watch by U.S. military (Courtesy of the 27th Army Division, National Archives, 1944)

Copyright ©2019 Stephanie Soder and Jennifer McKinnon. All rights reserved. Published by East Carolina University Foundation.
ISBN 978-0-9758874-5-5

It Rained Fire

Oral Histories from the Battle for Saipan

Written & Edited by
Stephanie Soder and
Jennifer McKinnon

THIS PROJECT WAS MADE POSSIBLE BY SUPPORT FROM THE

NORTHERN MARIANAS HUMANITIES COUNCIL

A NONPROFIT, PRIVATE CORPORATION FUNDED IN PART BY THE

NATIONAL ENDOWMENT FOR THE HUMANITIES

Acknowledgments

As is indicated in the forward, this project and resulting book came from a collective effort of the community. Great gratitude is owed to the Northern Marianas Humanities Council for funding the project.

A very special acknowledgment and thank you is owed to Genevieve Cabrera and Fred Camacho, who have been colleagues for many years and the impetus for continuing to consider and explore indigenous experiences in WWII. Their love of the land and sea and history of their islands is incomparable and shows in the trust they provide outside researchers who wish to learn about that history. Gen and Fred helped define the project through their knowledge of the camp locations, their identification of community elders willing to share their memories, and their assistance in collecting and helping with the review of those stories. Gratitude must also be extended to Madeline Roth, who volunteered to collect stories and data with the research team.

Finally, this book would not have been possible without the words on the pages spoken by the survivors and their families. Your ability to trust and share your memories and your commitment to recording those for future generations will be acknowledged and thanked for decades to come.

CONTRIBUTORS

Larry Cabrera
Luis Cabrera
Soledad Cabrera
David Camacho
Michael Camacho
Marie Castro
Meling Chargualaf
Sister Asuncion "Chong" Demapan
Felix Fitial
Estanislao Fujihara
Juan Laffet
Thomasa Camacho Naraja
Julia Norita
Lino Olopai
Rosa "Chailang" Palacios
Gonzalo Pangelinan
Jesus Pangelinan
Rafaela Perry
Rafael Ilo Rangamar
Rita Reyes
Ben Sablan
Felix Sasamoto
Connie Togawa
Stanley Torres
Isabel Villagomez

FOREWORD

The Battle for Saipan was and still is one of the most impactful and tragic historical events to have touched the lives of indigenous Pacific Islanders in the Marianas. At least 933 indigenous people lost their lives and countless more were injured, lost their homes and personal economy, lost their families and friends, and were forced to relocate and then resettle a land that was already rightfully theirs. Yet despite the tragic nature of the battle and its immediate aftermath, there is a resilience that is indescribable and unmatched across the globe. While historians call it "history," it is by no means historical to those who live on the island today and share those memories with their families; it is very much a part of the present and future of the island.

Many stories have been collected and much history has been written about the warring forces in the battle for Saipan, yet the indigenous stories and memories have yet to be fully explored. This book attempts to add to and expand the collective memory of suffering and resilience of indigenous Pacific Island survivors and their family members through recording and sharing their voices.

This book is part of a larger project which draws on tenets of community archaeology and indigenous archaeology in that it is was conceived "by, for, and with" the community of the Northern Mariana Islands and centers the indigenous voice in the narrative of the past. The project was funded by a Northern Marianas Humanities Council grant and several community members assisted with the design, collection, transcription, and review of the project and data. As such, this book is a community effort and belongs to those who are the keepers of these stories. We hope that you enjoy reading these stories in the words of your own family, friends, and neighbors.

JAPANESE ADMINISTRATION

The Japanese administration on Saipan began following the Treaty of Versailles in 1918, when the League of Nations officially allocated all German Pacific assets north of the equator to Japan. Under a Class C mandate, the Japanese government was required to continue many of the programs created by the previous German administration, including schooling, building island infrastructure, and establishing laws.

The Japanese armed forces left the island under the care of the South Seas Government in 1922, and with that, came the Nan'yō Kōhatsu Kabushiki Kaisha (NKK).

The NKK primarily focused on developing the industry on the island, with special interest in sugarcane manufacturing and the island fisheries. Instead of employing the indigenous civilians, however, the NKK encouraged emigration of Japanese and other foreign civilians onto the island. This decision ensured that the Japanese expanded their empire into the Pacific Islands while also keeping their livelihood away from indigenous hands, citing "the native's ability to work in modern industrial enterprises was very poor." The time under the Japanese administration brought about changes to the island that deeply impacted the indigenous civilians, in both positive and negative ways.

The sugarcane industry utilized Korean workers, while the commercial fishing industry employed Okinawan civilians. Within years, the foreign population dwarfed the indigenous populations on the island. While many of the indigenous civilians admit to a complicated relationship with the Japanese, their relationships with emigrants was much more favorable. According to Chailang Palacios:

> **"The one thing my father told us was that the Japanese trained them how to farm and how to build their cement houses. But he really wasn't pleased with the Japanese. The Okinawans were the best friends of the Chamorro and Carolinians, they were workers for the Japanese. The Japanese were first-class, and they looked down on us."**

The Nan'yō Kōhatsu Kabushiki Kaisha sugar mill and railroad, circa 1930s.
Courtesy of the University of Hawaii

Street view of Garapan, the "Tokyo of the South", circa 1930s.
Courtesy of the CNMI Historic Preservation Office

Luis Cabrera recalls:

"The Japanese were very kind to the local people. They occupied all of the local property and the local people were making money left and right. The Japanese had invested in the island. Tapioca manufacturing, sugar cane manufacturing, cotton planting, tuna canning, you name it."

Infrastructure continued to grow and multiple industries on Saipan became profitable for the Japanese government. The city of Garapan was even considered the "Tokyo of the South" due to its bustling nature, becoming the regional epicenter of Japanese sophistication.

Under the League of Nations mandate, the Japanese administration was required to provide schooling for the indigenous civilians. One civilian, wishing to remain anonymous, recalls the school system being more than adequate; the students were provided school supplies and food for free. According to Chailang Palacios, her sister had wanted to go to Japanese school but was not allowed beyond third grade. Instead, the Mercedarian nuns taught her to be a homemaker and wife.

Despite a satisfactory curriculum, the teachers at the school were remembered as being extremely strict. Civilian Marie Castro remembers:

"When I was in the Japanese school, my friend next to me didn't understand the instruction and she turned to me and whispered to ask for information. The teacher caught her talking to me, she called the student up and she took the scissors and cut her eyelashes. That student couldn't open her eyes for weeks and the mother was furious about it, but that was one of the punishments. Another time, I remember during the raising of the flag, you have to stand immobile just like the military. And this young man, I think he was in the fifth grade, a mosquito was on his nose during the raising of the flag. He tried to remove it and the teacher caught him doing that. They punished him by making him stand under the flagpole the whole day. No restroom, no lunch, nothing. I remember seeing the sister of that boy that was punished, she was crying."

The strict nature extended beyond school as well. Rafaela Perry, born just before the battle, recalls her parents telling her:

"If you do something wrong, the Japanese might smack you in the back of the head. They said working hours are working hours, and playing time is playing time, there's no foolishness of in between."

The treatment of the indigenous civilians likely stemmed from the hierarchy of race within Japanese culture. In their eyes, mainland Japanese were first-class citizens, followed by Okinawan civilians and Korean civilians. Because all Micronesian civilians fell outside the cultural and geographic limits of Asia, indigenous civilians on Saipan were seen as the lowest class, unable to be true imperial subjects.

Any positive relationships cultivated between Japanese and indigenous civilians began to dissipate in the late 1930s. As tension grew between the Japanese empire and western powers, the treatment of indigenous, Okinawan, and Korean civilians began to worsen as time passed.

Garapan (below) was one of two major villages on Saipan. Chalan Kanoa, located south of Garapan, was the other major village.
Courtesy of the CNMI Historic Preservation Office

The Japanese military became extremely suspicious of the indigenous civilians and their attitude towards them became more strict and violent. The Japanese military established a curfew for indigenous civilians, many of whom complied rather than risk being assaulted. Juan Laffet recalls:

> "My brothers did tell me once that they were playing with a toy telephone and the Japanese took it and yelled at them because they thought they were communicating with the Americans."

Once the war in the Pacific began, the Japanese military poured onto the island. With no extra space for the influx of soldiers, indigenous civilians were forced out of their houses in order to accommodate the Japanese military. Fortunately, many of the indigenous civilians had homesteads and farms away from Garapan and were able to find safety away from the soldiers. Those that did not have a farm were forced to move into caves. Thomasa Naraja recalls:

> "The family compound was taken and occupied by the Japanese soldiers, so my mom and dad moved all thirteen of us children to a cave. We didn't have any water in the cave, and when my dad and sister went to the school nearby to get some, they were threatened by the Japanese."

Japanese military members on Saipan prior to the battle, 1944. Courtesy of the Col. James A Donovan Collection

Further actions by the Japanese military resulted in forced, unpaid labor by the indigenous civilians. Marie Castro remembers:

> "After we had moved to the farm, the Japanese ordered for all the men who were living in the northern part of the island to be transferred to the southern part to work and for those who were living in the south to be transferred to the north. The family was completely cut from the father because of this. And I remember my mother was so devastated with the feeling of having to be both roles, the mother and then the father. She didn't know anything about fishing or going and getting something for us to live."

Indigenous children were also forced to work. The United States (U.S.) military began dropping bombs on Saipan in the early months of 1944, specifically near the airfield around the Kagman area. Luis Cabrera remembers how students were no longer taught anything in school, and instead, were forced to work on the airfield.

The U.S. military's main interests focused on Saipan's strategic location, resources available, and economic importance to Japan. Saipan, located approximately 1,500 miles southeast of Japan and 3,200 miles west from Hawai'i, was targeted specifically as a mid-way point to refuel long-range bomber planes on their way to Japan. As the U.S. did not have any other foothold in the Pacific that could allow for their planes to stop for refueling, Saipan's location was of utmost importance. Furthermore, the Japanese military had constructed airstrips on Saipan, as well as Tinian, Rota, Pagan, and Guam. The U.S. planned to utilize these airstrips once gaining a position in the Marianas. Securing Saipan would also deal a devastating blow to the Japanese economy, as they had invested heavily in the island's sugarcane industry and commercial fishing.

There are many different views regarding the level of information being passed down to the indigenous civilians concerning the approaching battle. With the influx of Japanese military on the island and the early bombings of 1944, civilians that were older at the time remember knowing that a war was coming to the island. Stanley Torres recollects:

> "Before the war started here, we already knew that the Americans were coming. My parents, when they see a plane, they know it's American."

Similarly, Meling Chargualaf states:

> "My brother remembers when the American ships came in, he was saying how exciting it was. They looked like little toys. But then everyone started running, and things got serious, because they were starting to bomb us."

Others recall that they knew that the Japanese were at war with someone but did not know who they were fighting. Thomasa Naraja explains:

> "The war wasn't a complete surprise to us because soldiers were on the island, but we didn't know who the war was with or how it was going. One Japanese soldier was trying to tell us about the war, but the concept of 'war' was so foreign to us."

Those that were children at the time recall not knowing what was going on, but understanding that something was happening to make everyone uneasy. The battle itself came as a surprise. Julia Norita remembers:

> "I was only seven when the war began. We didn't know the war was coming; we only knew it was a problem when the air raid sirens were on and the Japanese were announcing to seek shelter and to hide. That's when we knew there were going to be problems. Once the sirens went off, my father gathered up the family and we took off towards a cave up the hill. And that's when the bombardment started."

On 12 June 1944, the U.S. military began bombarding the island of Saipan, sending the civilians on the island running for shelter in caves and water cisterns. Those that did not seek shelter were caught in the crosshairs of battle as the U.S. military began their invasion.

The Battle For Saipan

For those that knew of the U.S. military's impending arrival, preparations were made in order to ensure their survival. Families stocked caves and other shelters near their homesteads with goods such as food, fresh water, and clothing, and some even buried their valuables in the hope that if they survived, they would be able to retrieve them. Sister Asuncion "Chong" Demapan recounts:

"My father and mother had prepared a cave for our family beforehand with breadfruit, water, food that wouldn't spoil, and clothing. Around four o'clock in the afternoon, people began shouting and the sirens started up; my parents told us to follow them."

Similarly, Chailang Palacios recounts the story her sister told her about her own family's experience with the day the battle began:

"I was born in 1941, so I was still very young and I don't really remember the war. We were up at our relative's place, the Tudela family, for my uncle's wedding in Dandan. There was so much food on the table; delicious pigs, chicken, fish, rice, taro, breadfruit, banana. And they were getting ready to pray, and all of a sudden, my sister said "Oh my god, it's raining like fire!" Everybody was so scared, they abandoned the food at the table and they all ran away. We had a cave ready with banana leaf just in case there's war and was prepared for maybe twelve people. And they ended up with around thirty."

Early bombardment of the island by the U.S. focused on the villages of Garapan and Chalan Kanoa, as well as a few Japanese military fortifications. American poet John Ciardi, who came to Saipan during the war as a B-29 gunner, later

A street view of Garapan after the U.S. bombardment, June 1944.
Courtesy of the 27th Army Division

ommented, "Garapan in Saipan and Agana in Guam are the two most completely destroyed towns I have ever seen." Luis Cabrera remembers the U.S. ships off the coast of Saipan:

> "Because we were on the high area, we could see all of the ships surrounding the area. The battleship, destroyer, the minesweeper, all of them. I wasn't really scared because I didn't understand what was going on. Then when they suddenly started to bomb the area, that's when my family got scared. My mother, father, brothers, sisters, auntie, grandmother and grandfather- my whole family, we all ran to the cave near where we lived."

Fortunately, most of the indigenous civilians were away from town at this point, either out at their homesteads or taking shelter. Those that had not prepared were also able to take temporary shelter in above-ground concrete water cisterns.

On 15 June 1944, the U.S. military landed on Saipan under the direction of Admiral Raymond A. Spruance. This would be

The village of Garapan after the U.S. military bombardment, June 1944. Courtesy of the 27th Army Division

U.S. Army reinforcements making their way to the beach from the LSTs on the reef, 1944. Courtesy of the 27th Army Division

the first time that the U.S. military engaged with an indigenous civilian population alongside Japanese civilians and soldiers. In light of this predicament, the U.S. military proposed to distribute propaganda leaflets to target all groups on the island, including the Chamorro and Carolinians.

These propaganda texts were written in Japanese Katakana and stated that the U.S. military would not harm or kill civilians. It further promised food, water, clothing, and tobacco to those that surrendered at the U.S. frontlines and did not assist any Japanese military members along the way. A "Life-Saving Guarantee" was attached to the pamphlet that civilians were to submit to U.S. military service members; on the back of this guarantee, English instructions for the soldiers were also printed to ensure that the treatment of civilians conformed to the Geneva Convention.

While U.S. military records from interrogations with indigenous civilians claim that the propaganda leaflets were well-received with many civilians ready to follow the instructions, others note that most did not see the leaflets.

Most indigenous civilians stayed within their shelters until the end of the battle. Unfortunately, this did not ensure their complete safety. As U.S. military forces made their way across the island, firefights erupted between them and the Japanese, often catching civilians in the crossfire. Connie Togawa remembers:

"I was very young when the war came to Saipan, about five years old. I remember some of it, and my father and mother told us stories as well. My father built a cave in Chalan Piao so that we would have somewhere to hide. My mother and father would bring water and food inside the cave. And it wasn't only us, there were two other families that joined us. While my auntie Carmen was carrying my sister on her back, she was wounded very badly. They were both hurt, but my auntie was the serious one. I also got wounded from burning embers while I was pointing up at the sky."

Stories such as this are common. Estanislao Fujihara recalls:

"My stepmother did tell me that when the bombardment started, there had been no preparation and so we just hid in a cave or tunnel. My father was carrying two of my sisters to safety when he was hit by bullets, and all three died. They are buried in Chalan Kanoa."

Rita Reyes, born after the war, was told by her parents how they survived through battle, and about the siblings that she was never able to meet:

"Once the Americans came, my family moved into a tunnel in Gualo Rai. We hadn't been able to prepare anything, and we had to move from one place to another. My baby brother, who was born one week before the invasion started, died during the battle. My brother, sister, and father were all struck by bullets too. My sister died from her wounds."

The landscape of Saipan was completely decimated during the battle, as shown in this photograph. A column of smoke rises from Tanapag Harbor. Courtesy of the 27th Army Infantry Division

The caves may have offered some level of protection from aerial bombardment, but it could not protect those inside from bullet ricochets, flame throwers, and the Japanese military. In some cases, Japanese soldiers removed the indigenous civilians from their caves in order to take the supplies inside or take shelter themselves. As a child, Larry Cabrera remembers his family being removed from their cave so that a Japanese soldier could commit *gyokusai* or "honorable death" inside. One woman, who wished to remain anonymous, spoke about her family's encounter with a Japanese soldier:

"We made our way north towards Marpi to hide. We had not prepared a cave at all, and there were eight people total in the cave- my two parents and six children. Because my dad was Japanese, my brother had to go out to forage for food. We were so afraid for him. We moved between two caves when bombardment slowed down, and we ended up near San Juan near Kalabera Cave. As we were heading to a new cave, a Japanese soldier came upon us. He grabbed my father and pulled out his sword. He ordered my father to behead the entire family. My father told him no, that he was Catholic, and told the soldier that he was the enemy. He then shoved the Japanese soldier out of the cave, and somehow, a bomb went off and killed him instantly."

The indigenous civilians largely describe their time in the caves as fearful and devastating. Those that had prepared caves did not anticipate how long they would have to stay in the caves or could not account for the amount of people that took shelter with them. This led to supplies running out quickly, leaving civilians with no choice but to leave the safety of the caves to forage for food and fresh water.

Bombardment by the U.S. and the use of flamethrowers left the island landscape decimated with very little flora and fauna remaining. Hungry and thirsty, civilians went through great lengths to survive on any resources that were available. Stanley Torres recalls:

"My dad would sneak out during the nighttime to get sticks of sugarcane. My mother told me that when I was in the cave, I was crying because of thirst. So my dad would chew the sugarcane and put his mouth to my mouth and transfer that sugarcane juice to me. That's how they kept me quiet because the Japanese were patrolling the area and if they hear a baby crying, they would come in and yell or they would kill the baby. My parents were afraid of them."

As the U.S. military made their way across the island, skirmishes between the Japanese became frequent, putting the indigenous civilians at risk. Courtesy of the 27th Army Division

Often, the only remaining food sources were coconut, banana leaves, and sugarcane that had not been burned. Freshwater springs and rain provided enough to help some civilians survive, but others were desperate enough to drink water from the ocean. Many civilians spent weeks in these conditions, only leaving their cave shelter at night to avoid contact with Japanese and U.S. military.

As the U.S. military made their way across the island, interaction between the two groups became inevitable. Contact by the U.S. military with the indigenous civilians was often tense and fueled by fear. Prior to the battle, the Japanese military had told the indigenous that the U.S. military would torture and kill them if they were captured.

The inability to see one another further stressed these situations. The U.S. military did not enter any cave unless they were able to ensure that no Japanese soldiers hid inside, which could not be done unless they could see directly in the cave. Japanese interpreters could not accompany all units, and even if the indigenous heard the Japanese language, they would hesitate to come out. Because the Chamorro language borrows words from the Spanish language, some Spanish-speaking U.S. servicemen were able to communicate better. If civilians did not exit the cave, the U.S. military sometimes moved onto more violent means of clearing caves, such as flame throwers, grenades, or intermittent rifle firing.

To combat this issue, some indigenous civilians placed religious icons outside of their caves to show that they were Catholic, and therefore, not Japanese. If the civilians and U.S. military were able to see each other, they turned to gesturing to communicate.

Indigenous civilians speaking with U.S. military personnel as they leave the caves.
Courtesy of the National Archives

One civilian, wishing to remain anonymous, recounted:

> "The Americans eventually found us. We couldn't understand them, but knew they were Americans. You can imagine to laugh and to cry at the same time. My mom and dad yelled "We're Catholic!" and they stopped. When they heard the Chamorro [language], they said 'Come, come!' and the captain blew a whistle and told them to put down their guns."

Trust between the two groups was also stunted by the race of the soldiers. For many civilians on Saipan, this was the first time seeing a white or black person, as many had not lived through the German administration on the island. Some refused to leave their cave if the soldier trying to get them out was black, until they were out of food and water and had no other choice.

Fortunately, not all first interactions between the two groups were stressful. Rafaela Perry recalls the story her parents told her about their first contact with a U.S. Marine:

> "I was born on June 5, 1944, ten days before the invasion of Saipan. My family lived in Chalan Kiya, and when the war came, my dad took us all in a bull cart to a cave behind China Town, also known as Falipi. Later on, when the bombing stopped and we were still at the cave, an American marine found us. I'm not sure how they communicated, but they told me that he asked what my name was and my parents told him I don't have a name yet. He wanted me to be named after him, and they said this cannot be because it's a girl! So they named me Rafaela because his name was Raphael. They changed the spelling like the Spanish way. From there on, my family told me, he always came and visited me, bringing me milk from the military galley every time. He also wanted to hold and carry me, but my family was afraid that he might kidnap me. The family was also afraid that if they didn't allow him to carry me, then he might kill them. So with their eyes watching every move he made, they let him hold me. I would like to find Mr. Raphael's family and to share my story with them. I'm so thankful because I believe that from what he did, he saved me."

Once safe contact was initiated, the U.S. military moved all civilians that they encountered to temporary stockades with the 2nd and 4th Marine Divisions, and the 27th Army Infantry Division. If the language barrier was not a problem, the U.S. military would begin interviewing the civilians out in the field. The civilians were provided food, water, and medical aid at these sites, but safety was not guaranteed.

Military Police stand guard and pass out rations to a group of civilians while waiting for removal to the internment camp. Courtesy of the 27th Army Division

After leaving the cave her family stayed with the U.S. military, Marie Castro remembers:

"They took us up on a hill, walking. As we stayed up on the hill, the Americans were already interviewing the nuns and the priests. Sister Angelica knew Japanese and I think it was Guy Gabaldon who was interviewing the nuns. Another sister knew English, she was speaking in that. While we were up there on the hill, I looked up and it just seemed like the door of heaven opened for us. We were so free just to get the breeze, it was so nice. And then all of a sudden, they ordered us to lay down on the ground, close our eyes and ears. For about five minutes, we didn't know what was going on. After the incident was done, they explained what happened.

There were two Japanese trucks coming over to find the Americans. So from the top of the hill and from the ships, they just bombed the area and in five minutes everything was over."

The first civilians encountered were moved from the individual division stockades to one larger temporary stockade on the beach. This area contained very little shelter and resources but was far from the battle front. As more civilians came under the custody of the U.S. military complications arose at every turn.

Having anticipated that civilians would be on the island during the battle, the U.S. established a Civil Affairs unit to take charge of maintaining civilian order, both indigenous and foreign. These tasks included removal of indigenous civilians and their belongings from combat zones into safe areas, distribution of relief supplies, provision of medical aid, and establishing sanitation in these safe areas. They were also in charge of organizing civilian labor groups to assist with burial of the dead, supply and equipment distribution, and other duties as assigned. Interviews were to be conducted to provide counter intelligence to the military and records, public documentation, all government and civilian property, and enemy funds and supplies were to be seized. Finally, the Civil Affairs unit was to ensure that civilians were informed of their rights and duties under the military government.

According to Brigadier General G.B. Erskine, relief supplies and medical aid were to be given to internees "to meet minimum standards of occupied territory" and that any captured enemy goods, such as clothing, food, or supplies would be "conserved in order to facilitate re-establishment of law and order among the civilian population."

Unfortunately, the Civil Affairs section was unprepared for the complications that came from the aerial and naval bombardment of the island. It was initially believed that most of the structures on the island would remain untouched during the invasion; these assumptions led to a lack of pre-battle planning, in which the need for many resources was incorrectly calculated. In Major General Harry Schmidt's report:

> "The performance of the Civil Affairs section at the target indicated serious weakness in training. This section was in no sense prepared to meet and solve the harsh physical problems of sanitation, shelter, food, clothing and medical aid. The staff was well informed on the intricacies of city government, but it was helpless in the face of arduous field conditions, where thousands of civilians, homeless, starving, naked, wounded and in most cases terror-stricken by the savage fighting taking place but a few hundred yards away, suddenly appeared and clamored for assistance."

On 6 July 1944, the Civil Affairs unit took over the temporary stockades. It was quickly determined that the stockades on the beach were unsuitable due to their location, lack of shelter, and distance from resources. Major General Schmidt went on to report that the stockades were overcrowded and the "most primitive sort of temporary holding camps" constructed of tarpaulins and salvaged material that proved "totally inadequate."

Saipan was considered secured on 9 July 1944, though a number of Japanese holdouts remained at large for several months afterwards. At the end of the battle, 933 indigenous civilian casualties would be recorded due to the battle and internment; while this number does not seem high in respect to the almost 55,000 total casualties of battle, it was approximately one-quarter of the total indigenous population.

As the majority of the fighting had been completed, the Civil Affairs unit turned their attention to the civilian living situation. A larger, permanent camp was planned, and by 12 July 1944, all civilians were moved from the beach towards the western side of Lake Susupe. This camp was known as Internment Camp No. 1 to the U.S. military, but to the civilians, it was called Camp Susupe.

INTERNMENT

For the civilians on Saipan, Camp Susupe was a complex experience. Shell-shocked, injured, and suffering from lack of food and water, Camp Susupe was a place of potential refuge for most people. But in exchange for safety, the indigenous civilians had to give up their freedom. The military ensured the civilians protection by placing barbed wire fences around the entire camp, restricting movement into and out of camp, and guarding the area at all times.

At this time, the U.S. military was still searching the island for both civilians and Japanese holdouts. After Camp Susupe was established, all civilians were directly transported there by military truck; for some, this was the first time they had been in a vehicle or had seen a truck of this size. As soon as the civilians stepped into Camp Susupe, each was registered. A photograph was taken, an identification number was given, and all information was printed on a card for the civilian to carry.

By 15 July 1944, the U.S. military calculated a total of 13,289 interned civilians, including 2,258 Chamorro and 782 Carolinians. Less than two weeks later, the total jumped to 17,265 internees in Camp Susupe, with 2,308 Chamorro and 815 Carolinians.

Because all civilians were finally being directed to one location, this allowed for families and friends to reunite with one another. David Camacho, whose family was split up prior to the battle, fondly remembers:

"They took us to Camp Susupe in the back of the truck. When we got there, we were actually reunited with my twin brothers and aunties! That was a good time."

All civilians, including indigenous, were brought to Camp Susupe in the backs of U.S. military trucks. Courtesy of the National Archives

The Mercedarian Sisters and Capuchin Priests on Saipan after being brought to Camp Susupe, July 1944. Courtesy of the 27th Army Division

The safe return of the priests and nuns of the island caused further celebration. Marie Castro, who stayed with them during the battle, recalls:

"When we arrived in Camp Susupe, there were a lot of people. Everybody was excited when they saw the white uniform of the nuns. They said "Oh there are the nuns! They are safe!" Some of them were crying, others were praying, others were just so jubilant about the whole thing. It was really relief for the Chamorros to learn that the missionaries were safe. Here on Saipan, they were like our fathers and mothers."

Once the initial relief of reunification wore off, the realities of refugee life came swiftly for those in Camp Susupe. The civilians in the camp, unable to leave, had to completely rely on the U.S. military for supplies. Though initially unprepared to deal with the large number of civilians in need, the U.S. military was able to provide C-rations, salvaged food, and freshwater to those in camp. The tents and tarpaulins from the beach stockade were reutilized to create shared shelters. As a child in Camp Susupe, Larry Cabrera remembers:

> "The military was providing food to the civilians because there was no more warehouse, no store, no nothing. The military rationed food to families, and the amount of food was inadequate. I don't know how long we were there, but I believe the camp was getting too large because the people were being found in caves or came out from hiding. The place was crowded."

With over 17,000 civilians in one place, the same problems that occurred in the beach stockades began to occur in Camp Susupe. The area was overcrowded, hot, and unsanitary; mosquitos swarmed the camp daily.

As conditions worsened, so did temperaments. At the time, all civilians were together in Camp Susupe, including Japanese civilians. As tension grew, the groups were separated from one another. Families of mixed ethnicity could stay together in the indigenous civilian section.

Indigenous families took shelter under tarps and other salvaged material, with many sleeping on the bare ground. Courtesy of the Steward Collection

A Chamorro family inside of their make-shift shelter, made from palm fronds. Courtesy of the U.S. Air Force

Civilians wait in line in order to recieve vaccinations, Camp Susupe 1944. Courtesy of the 27th Army Division

Camp Susupe bathing and laundry washing area. Courtesy of the U.S. Navy

One man, wishing to remain anonymous, was a teenager when he and his family were placed in Camp Susupe. He recounts:

> "The Chamorros and Carolinians were put together into one group, and the Japanese, Okinawans, mixed, and Koreans were in another because of tension. There was a form of continual war where a Chamorro would see a Japanese that he recognized as someone that did them harm or was boastful, and they would go over to the Japanese and hurt them. The Military Police would allow us to go up to them, they wouldn't stop it. The Japanese would bow down and ask for forgiveness. And it wouldn't just happen in camp, when we were sent out to the farm in the Chalan Kiya area, it would happen."

For most civilians, there are two different perspectives of Camp Susupe. In the eyes of some civilians, they found safety and a sense of control once coming to camp after a terrifying war took place. Marie Castro believes:

> "We were protected with barbed wire around so that Japanese snipers would not be coming in. It was guarded. Camp Susupe was a safe haven for us. They gave us medicine, food, everything that the Americans could provide for us."

Others, however, remember Camp Susupe as a dismal place. Soledad Cabrera recalls:

> "I remember Camp Susupe. We slept under a green tent on a cot. I remember the barbed wire fence all around- we felt like prisoners."

Similarly, Thomasa Naraja recalls:

"At Camp Susupe, I remember the barbed wire fence around us. We were placed into tents, given cots, and had a kitchen area. They gave us canned hash for food. I worked as a nurse with the 2nd Marine Division, helping soldiers that were hurt in the battle. My three-month-old sister died while in Camp Susupe."

Carpenters from the 47th and 805th Army Engineers slowly added semi-permanent structures to the existing camp, including 150 20'x40' shelters built from salvaged material. Unfortunately, while the shelters improved, living conditions did not.

Overcrowding and the tension between the civilian groups ultimately led to the decision by the U.S. military to expand Camp Susupe into the nearby village of Chalan Kanoa.

An aerial view of Camp Susupe. The large structures were built by U.S. military carpenters after civilians spent months living in make-shift shelters.
Courtesy of the National Archives

In October 1944, in an area that was being used by the U.S. military for shelter, Seabee and Army carpenters began refurbishing pre-war concrete houses that had survived through the battle. Chamorro and Carolinian families began moving into the area as early as November 1944, providing relief for all groups within Camp Susupe. Although it was still an internment camp with barbed wire surrounding the village, this area would simply be called Chalan Kanoa.

Chalan Kanoa was divided into four separate sections based on ethnicity, though it is unclear whether this division was organized by the military or the civilians themselves. District 1 was located on the northeast corner of Chalan Kanoa and provided housing for multi-ethnic and Chamorro families. District 2, located on the northwest side of the village, was designated for Chamorro families and eventually northern islanders, with several families from Chuuk, Jaluit, and Yap. District 3 was located in the southeastern section of Chalan Kanoa and comprised almost entirely of Chamorro families.

District 4, located in the southwest corner of the village next to the beach, was mainly utilized by the Carolinian families. As such, the district was given the slang term "Lally Four" (spelled phonetically) by Carolinian youth; "Lally" in Carolinian is translated as "that's it," though the exact meaning of the name is unknown. These districts were not strictly segregated, though some civilians felt that this separation occurred to prevent any further tension in the new camp.

The first families to move into Chalan Kanoa were placed into the pre-war NKK concrete houses. There were not enough houses for each family to have their own, which meant that two or three families shared each house. Some civilians added dividers to create separate spaces for each family, though some civilians remember one large room to share. In some cases, families were able to share houses with relatives or family friends. Meling Chargualaf, who still lives in the house her family was placed into during internment, recalls:

> "The Americans put us in this house. It was originally divided, and we shared it with another family we were related to. There were so many kids in here though. My parents had seven kids, and the other Cabrera family had five, I think. So there were twelve kids in this house!"

As soon as all of the concrete houses were inhabited, military carpenters and civilians began to build wooden duplex and triplex houses. Eventually, each family would have a house to themselves, though it would take almost the entire time they were interred.

As time went on, the food provided to the civilians became better in both quantity and quality. The U.S. military provided ration boxes to the civilians, though they were no longer the C-rations given to them in Camp Susupe. Ration boxes included canned meat, rice, powdered milk, bread, and powdered eggs.

One of the wooden houses built by carpenters in Chalan Kanoa, 1944.
Courtesy of the U.S. Navy

These ration boxes were further supplemented by fresh vegetables and fruit from farms cultivated by the civilians. Larry Cabrera describes how he spent his childhood in Chalan Kanoa:

> "People were still locked in the camp, but somebody finally had the idea to turn the people loose so that we could fend for ourselves. They gathered up all the farmers and got them to start farming. I was too young to go to school, so I went to work with my father at the farm. We'd go out every day with other farmers and plant tapioca, sweet potatoes, okra, green onions, stuff like that. The produce from the farm helped with the food rationing and helped the people to have enough food. I also helped my mom around the house. I would go get the rations from the store. I remember Thanksgiving was a fun day at the ration store because everyone gets turkey. They divvied them among families, maybe a half turkey for each family."

Along with the fresh produce from the farms came fish caught by the Carolinians in District 4. Fishing gear owned by the indigenous civilians had been destroyed during the battle, including boats.

The main gate of Chalan Kanoa, 1945. Courtesy of the National Archives

This is the building where ration boxes were distributed to each family. Rations often consisted of dried and canned goods, and were supplemented with fresh produce from the farms and fishing vessels. Courtesy of the U.S. Air Force

With their strategic location next to the beach, Carolinians used spears and nets to catch unicorn fish, salmon, tuna, carp, guili (rudderfish) and gadao (grouper). They mostly stayed inside the reef to fish, with records showing that Okinawans used refurbished boats to fish under military supervision in deeper water. Lack of materials and restrictions for leaving camp meant that boatbuilding, a common craft among Carolinians, could not be completed. Fishermen would often communally share their catch with immediate family and neighbors, but also bartered for other supplies with their extra fish.

Net making, among other handicraft projects, became a social activity to help pass time while in camp. Turtles, fish, and miniature boats were often the subject of woodcarvings created by indigenous civilians. Furniture, hats, sandals, religious icons, woven art and other crafts were also created by the indigenous civilians for extra money. The creations were sold to the U.S. military in the Handicraft Store, which overall proved to be a lucrative venture. A Civil Affairs report from July 1945 claims that the indigenous and Japanese handicraft cooperatives produced $5,116.20 of goods in that month alone.

The handicraft cooperative was just one of many ways in which the indigenous civilians could make money in camp.

Employment opportunities were provided by the U.S. military, and civilians were paid for both skilled and unskilled labor. Most civilians remember their parents working for the military in some capacity. One civilian, wishing to remain anonymous, recalls the work that her parents did in Chalan Kanoa:

> "My dad worked for 20 cents an hour. For extra money, he would carve religious figurines, shoes and sandals, and chairs and other furniture. My mother worked for the military as a housekeeper for $1.50 per day. Back then, $1 could buy three canned goods at the store that they opened."

Other civilians, both men and women, remember working as administrative assistants, truck drivers, seamstresses, custodians, laundry workers, cooks, teachers, and tradesmen. Early reports from the U.S. military express their belief that the Chamorro and Carolinian attitudes were "very much against the Japanese and favorable to the United States. They are willing and cooperative and as soon as it is safe for them to return to their former occupations they should be allowed to do so."

An indigenous police force was created in order to replace the military guards around Camp Susupe and Chalan Kanoa. When the changeover first occurred, early military reports stated "gratifyingly, substitution of the native guards resulted in an actual increase in orderliness among internees." By June 1945, the Civil Affairs unit reported a total of 114 Chamorro police officers.

Above: Indigenous farmers split the sweet potato crop for distribution.
Courtesy of the National Archives
Below: Civilians work as seamstresses in Chalan Kanoa. Courtesy of the U.S. Air Force

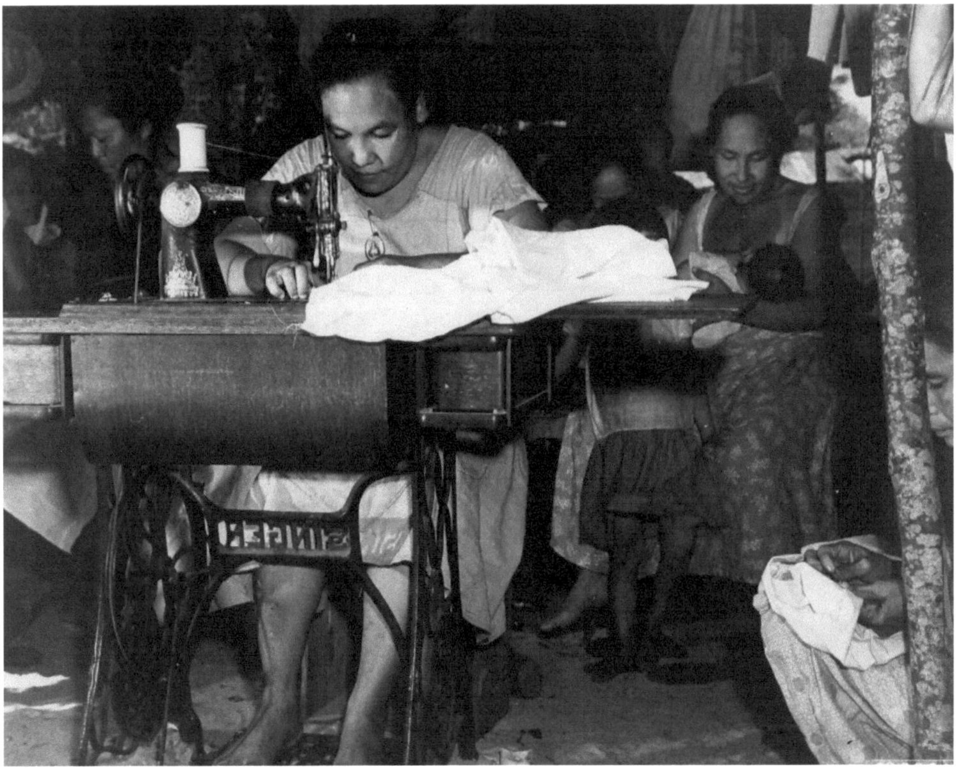

A Chamorro guard checks the identification of a U.S. soldier entering camp. Indigenous guards and police were in charge of both Chalan Kanoa and Camp Susupe, 1945. Courtesy of the U.S. Navy

Not only did allowing civilians to act as their own guards and police officers create a mutually respectful relationship between the U.S. military and indigenous civilians, but it also ensured the safety of civilians in the camp. Orders specifically prohibited soldiers from entering the camps unless on official business, and non-fraternization rules forbade personal relationships between military and civilians.

Norman Meller, a young U.S. naval officer, remembers how a fellow officer was arrested by the Chamorro police for violating the non-fraternization orders, even though his relationship with a Chamorro woman was approved by her family. Another recollection from Escolastica Tudela Cabrera detailed how Father Jose Tardio, one of the Spanish priests on the island, refused to marry a U.S. soldier to a Chamorro woman. Both the U.S. military and the indigenous civilians seemed to believe in keeping their distance from one another.

Despite these rules and limited access into camp, members of the U.S. military and indigenous civilians worked together outside of camp. Trust between the two groups grew, likely as a result of working side-by-side, and the U.S. military's opinion of indigenous civilians grew stronger every day. Because of the burgeoning relationships, the U.S. military decided to employ the use of indigenous scouts in Expedition APPLE, which commenced in July 1945.

Expedition APPLE focused primarily on contacting indigenous populations and securing Japanese surrender on neighboring islands, relying heavily on indigenous intelligence and translators.

The islands of Agrihan, Asuncion, Alamagan, Anatahan, Maug, Pagan, and Sarigan were all contacted by the U.S. military with the help of ten indigenous scouts, three indigenous interpreters, and one Japanese scout. Rafael Ilo Rangamar, as a 10-year-old boy living on the island of Asuncion with his family, remembers:

> "The Navy arrived on our island in 1945. Ed Peters, another Carolinian, was dropped off at the south end of the island and came to us, telling us the Americans were coming. We all went to my grandmother's farm to await their arrival. Most of the Americans were black, they were very nice people and gave us C-rations and candy. The vessel that came on the island had the number 448 on the side. It left with the Japanese and Okinawans first, and went from Asuncion to Agrihan and Maug, and then came back to pick us up a week later. We stopped at Pagan, but everyone was already dead or evacuated. By the time we got to Saipan, the Chamorro and Carolinians were out of Camp Susupe and into Chalan Kanoa."

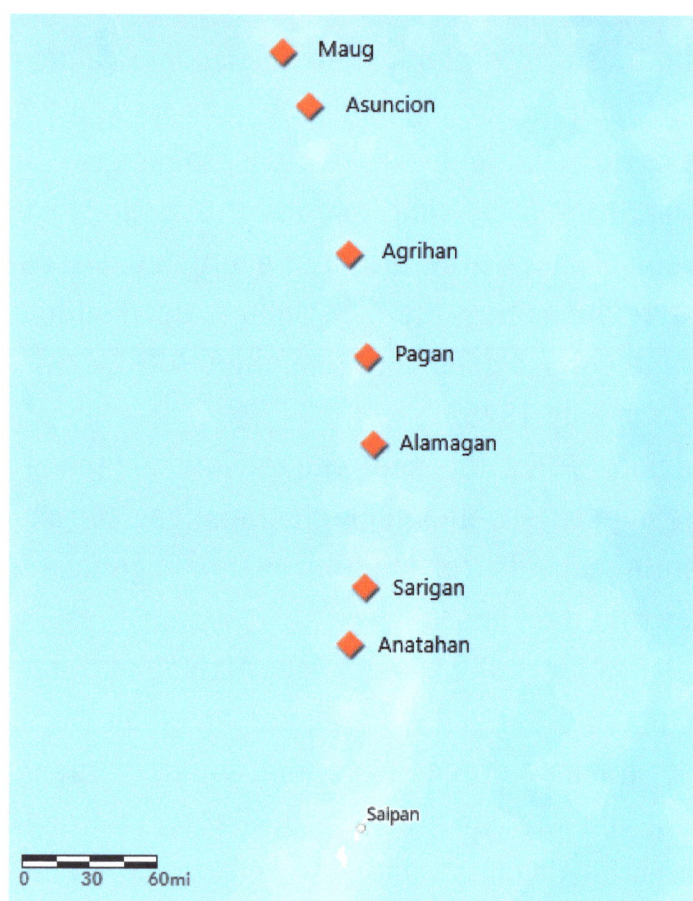

A map of the locations of the islands visited in Expedition APPLE in relation to Saipan

On the island of Alamagan, Jesus Pangelinan shares what life was like:

"I was born in 1942 on the island of Alamagan. My father was one of the men who constructed the Pagan airfield. It was continuously destroyed by an American plane, so they had to continue to repair it. The Japanese were very mean to us; they told us that we would be exterminated. My father also fished for the military, he used boats and spears to catch the fish. It's sugarcoating saying "we fished for them"- it was a demand. I remember looking out at the ocean and seeing the U.S. Navy warships. When the Americans came, about fifty of us from Alamagan, Pagan, and Anatahan were moved to Chalan Kanoa."

All civilians were removed from the islands and brought back to Saipan, where they were given housing in Chalan Kanoa in District 2.

The indigenous scouts and interpreters impressed the U.S. military so much that, in his operational report, Lieutenant R.C. Coburn praised the scouts for their knowledge of the terrain and courage. He further states:

> "The native scouts who went with this expedition rendered exceedingly valuable services and were used extensively by the Ground Forces in searching for Japanese...It is strongly recommended that a company of scouts be recruited among the young Chamorro and [Carolinian] men; that these young men be given a short course of instruction in the handling of American carbines or similar weapons and in the use of simple English terms; and that this company be used as an auxiliary unit to the American Armed Forces for such purposes as the elimination of Japanese from the Marianas and the prosecution of the Air Sea Rescue Program. The natives of Saipan have a strong attachment to the Second Marine Division, into whose lines they came during the invasion of Saipan."

These trips to the northern islands continued even after the end of the war. Felix Sasamoto, 4 years old when the U.S. military came to his home in Sarigan, remembers Elias Sablan and Gregorio Kilili acting as interpreters for the military and escorting everyone to Saipan. His father, who was Japanese, assisted on another mission to the northern islands in 1950.

He recalls:

> "Commander Johnson knew my father well and requested that he come with them on a mission to Anatahan because he speaks Japanese. They went to pick up an Okinawan woman [Kazuko Higa] that was left on the island with thirteen Japanese men after her husband died. They fought over her, and by the time the Americans went back to the island, there were only two men left."

Working together allowed the indigenous civilians to build positive relationships with the U.S. military, and overall, the interactions between the two groups are described as amicable. However, there were instances in which the U.S. military was described as less than good-natured. Some civilians recall a

Felix Sasamoto's father (second from the left) with the group of scouts under Commander Johnson. Kazuko Higa (middle) became known as the "Queen of Anatahan." Courtesy of Felix Sasamoto

story involving soldiers attempting to assault Chamorro women in farm fields. Those that recall such instances, however, stressed that they believe it to be a part of war and not indicative of the U.S. military overall.

The relationships between the U.S. military and indigenous children are consistently positive. Many civilians believed the soldiers to be especially attached to small children, likely due to feelings of homesickness. Those who were children at the time recall yelling to the soldiers, calling them "Joe" or "sindalu", meaning soldier in Chamorro. The military usually responded by sharing candy, apples, and other little gifts with the children, mostly from the other side of the camp boundary fence.

Lino Olopai, as a young Carolinian child, remembers fondly:

> "What I remember most from camp was that whenever the armed forces delivered water in that tank truck, us kids would run after those guys and they'd give us chocolate, candy, chewing gum. It was a big deal whenever we'd see them coming with the truck- we'd run and yell "Hey Joe!", and when they were done, they'd give us whatever they had. I'm sure it was hard on our parents during that time in camp, making sure we had food and water. But for me, you see all kinds of people in the camp and you hear the truck coming, so it was a fun day for us kids."

Schooling for children began as soon as they moved out of Camp Susupe. The civilians were not allowed to speak Japanese, therefore schooling focused primarily on English. The Chamorro and Carolinian languages were taught at home but were allowed to be spoken in school; children that were part of Japanese-Chamorro families usually spoke neither English or

Chamorro, making the transition difficult. The Chalan Kanoa school also taught mathematics and created a singing choir. The class system was not split by age like the modern system, but instead by how much the children already knew. Children were also required to take castor and codfish oil at school, as well as given vaccinations, memories that most civilians do not recall fondly.

Children that were too young to enter school kept busy in other ways. Many helped their parents by cleaning around the house, attending to the farms, fishing, or collecting ration boxes and water from the dispensary. Once chores were completed, most children elected to play outside. As a child living in Chalan Kanoa, Felix Fitial remembers:

> "I was too young to go to school, so I helped my mom and dad and siblings around the house with cooking, washing, and cleaning. I also played a lot of games like dodgeball, mancala, and baseball. Sometimes the Americans would play in Chalan Kanoa and hit the ball over the fence, and we would catch it and hide it so that we could play with the baseball!"

A group of young girls playing outside in Chalan Kanoa, 1945. Courtesy of the U.S. Navy

Left: Lt. McGown and Chief Steward Jesus pose with two civilians in Chalan Kanoa. Lt. McGown played Santa Claus for the children in Camp Susupe and Chalan Kanoa
Right: A young mother and her baby walk through Chalan Kanoa
Courtesy of the U.S. Navy

Civilians that described their childhood in Chalan Kanoa also remember chasing the military trucks through camp, playing in the ocean, and going to church. According to oral histories, the church was located where the Chalan Kanoa Post Office currently stands in the village.

As devout Catholics, many of the indigenous civilians went to church twice per day. The early church service was held around 5:30 a.m. every morning and the evening service was called Rosary. Rosary was often held by the altar servers and was a time to remember those that had died during the war and to celebrate their lives. Father Arnold Bendowski (Pale' Arnold in Chamorro), a Wisconsin-based priest who arrived on the island later, would pass out chocolate after Rosary.

According to many civilians, life in Chalan Kanoa was good. They were provided enough supplies to sustain comfortable lives and eventually, with the help of indigenous builders and military carpenters, many families lived in single-family homes. Electricity was even set up in some of the houses.

Civilian Connie Togawa reflects:

> "After moving to Chalan Kanoa, we did feel better, we were okay. We had a good life."

Not everybody felt this way, however. Benigno Sablan, who was very young at the time, recalls his own family's experience of Chalan Kanoa:

> "Those were the miserable times, because at those times, there was hardly anything to do, we were strange to the culture in Chalan Kanoa, strange to this place that we last lived, and we were always looking for food, foraging for food. War is a terrible thing."

By the time the Japanese surrendered on 2 September 1945, Chalan Kanoa felt more like a village than an internment camp for most. But despite the relationships cultivated between the U.S. military and the indigenous civilians, the end of the war did not mean the end of internment.

POST-WAR

After several long years of war, the Japanese Empire formally surrendered to U.S. forces on 2 September 1945 on the deck of U.S.S. *Missouri*. While the world rejoiced and cheered to the brokerage of peace, little changed on the island of Saipan. Civilians, both indigenous and foreign, remained behind barbed wire fences.

The U.S. military cited many reasons for keeping the internment camps running, the most prevalent of which was the presence of Japanese militants still at large around the island. Captain Sakae Oba, after rallying hundreds of Japanese civilians and soldiers, continued to lead attacks against the U.S. military on the island of Saipan. The indigenous civilians, aware of the situation, called these holdouts "snipers" or "stragglers." The stragglers continued to fire at civilians even after the end of the war. Captain Oba and those that remained of his group did not surrender until 1 December 1945.

The last holdouts on Saipan, surrendering on 1 December 1945.
Courtesy of the Attorney General

The surrender of Captain Oba still did not end the internment of indigenous civilians on Saipan. Repatriation of Japanese prisoners of war and foreign civilians became first priority for the U.S. government. Orders to deport all foreign nationals back to their home countries came on 15 September 1945, but movement on Saipan did not begin until the issue of island security was resolved.

In January 1946, Japanese prisoners of war began to be moved off island; further repatriation issues occurred, however, when the Commander of the Mariana Islands requested that workers be allowed to stay until January 1947. Foreign nationals who had lived on the island their entire lives even fought to stay on Saipan beyond the repatriation dates, arguing that Saipan was their only home.

Even after the security and repatriation issues were resolved, indigenous civilians continued to remain in Chalan Kanoa, and would continue to do so for another several months.

Captain Sakae Oba, "The Fox", on the day of his surrender. Courtesy of the Attorney General

Discussions had begun early regarding the management of the territory once held by the Japanese Empire. With the official surrender of Japan, the problem needed a resolution quickly. Two options lay on the table: continued military administration, or the implementation of a trusteeship in which the civilians would control their own administration. The creation of the United Nations in October 1945 quickly led to the United Nations Charter, and with that, an International Trusteeship System was arranged.

Arguments continued, however, regarding which entity would gain control and to what extent control would be exerted. On one side of the argument were people like Lieutenant John Useem of the U.S. Naval Reserve. Lt. Useem, who had worked several years in military administration of the Pacific, believed that the U.S. must assume some responsibility over the administration of the Pacific, but argued against complete control by a military unit.

In January 1946, Lt. Useem compiled a report offering his opinion that:

> "The basis for a sound administration of Micronesia can be stated in three general propositions. The first is indirect rule. The natives are fully capable of running their own internal affairs. The second is economic rehabilitation. The costly, inadequate relief program should be replaced by one in which the islanders regain economic self-dependency. This would entail an initial outlay for provisions to rebuild homes, industries, farming, and fishing. It also means re-establishment of a balanced money-economy, and orienting economic institutions to local needs. The Micronesians probably will never be completely self-sufficient, but by granting early tangible aid specifically designed to rebuild an integrated socio-economic system, demoralization can be avoided, the natives will be able to contribute a greater share of their own upkeep, and the cost to America will be far less over the years. The final need is for acculturation. This process has been under way for over a century, is taking place under American control, and it cannot be stopped. The task is, therefore, one of easing the adjustment and insuring that the best gestures of western civilization are disseminated without disrupting local social organization."

The other side of the argument called for complete control over the Pacific islands. One such argument stems from U.S. Lieutenant Commander T.O. Clark of the U.S. Naval Reserve.

In his April 1946 argument, he states:

> "To sum up briefly, my thesis is this. The price of the former Japanese mandated islands has been too high, and their value too great to ever relinquish. The United States Navy is the proper agency to colonize and administer these islands, utilizing almost entirely components already a part of the naval establishment. The concept attributed by Wallace to the Dutch, that native populations are in effect children and should be dealt with as such, should be the foundation of our policy in bringing the natives of these islands eventually to our own standard of living. When, as in the Philippines and the case of the Chamorros on Guam, natives show a high degree of receptivity, the civilizing process does not take long."

While these arguments continued, the civilians remained interned while their fate was decided for them. The Trust Territory of the Pacific Islands would not formally be approved by the United Nation's Security Council until 2 April 1947 and sanctioned by the U.S. until 18 July 1947.

Under the Trust Territory, Saipan, along with thousands of other Pacific Islands was placed in the care of the U.S. and protected under Chapter XII: International Trusteeship system, in which the U.S. was legally obligated to:

> "...promote the political, economic, social, and educational advancement of the inhabitants of the trust territories, and their progressive development towards self-government or independence as may be appropriate to the particular circumstances of each territory and its peoples and the freely expressed wishes of the peoples concerned, and as may be provided by the terms of each trusteeship agreement."

Since deliberations were progressing and details were beginning to be finalized, it was decided that Camp Susupe and Chalan Kanoa should be officially dissolved until a formal agreement could be made. On 4 July 1946, Saipan's indigenous civilians were cleared to move freely around the island, though with some stipulation. Luis Cabrera, a teenager at the time, recalls:

> "We were finally let go on July 4th. Any place you wanted to go, land, property, anywhere, you can go. That's why we celebrate Liberation Day. After that, we all went to Chalan Piao to our property before the war. We had to reestablish our house and our farm, and my father grew watermelons the size of Jeeps."

The flag raising ceremony on Liberation Day, 4 July 1946. Courtesy of the CNMI Historic Preservation Office

Lino Olopai, a six-year old Carolinian at the time of release, remembers:

> "After we were released from camp, there were six or seven fishing boats that were left on the island by the Okinawans. Several of the Carolinians became skipper of three or four boats that go out and catch tuna. So Saturday, when there was no school, I'd jump on with them and watch them catch tuna."

While some civilians left the Chalan Kanoa area, other families elected to stay in the houses that they owned in the village after the fences were removed. According to Meling Chargualaf, her family chose to stay in Chalan Kanoa instead of leaving:

> "After the war, the Cabrera family moved out to their compound in Chalan Piao, so my dad went to the Land Office and told them they moved out and they told us we could occupy the whole thing. I ended up staying here, breaking down the divided wall and making it one big house."

There were several factors that may have impacted a family's decision to stay or leave Chalan Kanoa. After the end of the war, the process of getting back to their pre-war land became extremely difficult for families.

Land records had been destroyed, if they had been kept at all, and the U.S. government decided that any land sold to the NKK or any other nationality prior to the war was now owned by the government, unless it could be proven that the indigenous person was forced to sell the property. This led to another restriction on indigenous civilians moving back to their own property: almost half of the island had been overtaken by the U.S. Navy.

The Naval Technical Training Unit (NTTU) was established on the northern side of the island, completely restricting access to the area. Indigenous civilians were strictly forbidden from entering the premises, unless employed by the NTTU and given authorization. Even being employed did not give total access to the area. Civilians could act as front gate security guards, carpenters, and laborers that worked on projects just outside the fenced area. Rafael Ilo Rangamar remembers his time working for the NTTU:

"When I was older, I got a job as a security guard with the NTTU. Ben Sablan came to my house and offered it to me. Covered trucks would be full of soldiers, transporting them from Marpi to Kagman. And before they came, the security officer would tell us that we should just let them through, no check."

Chailang Palacios, whose family moved just outside the perimeter fence, remembers:

"After we left Chalan Kanoa, we moved back up to our house in Marpi. We would stay there in the summer time and go back to Chalan Kanoa for school. Trucks would go past our house to go north where the NTTU was located, the backs full of soldiers. This was the time between World War II and the Korean War. We just prayed for no more war."

For many people on the island, there was a very active fear that another war would begin during the Cold War era. Civilians on the island still believe that the NTTU was a CIA base of operations; unfortunately, information is still classified regarding the activity in this area. Eventually, the NTTU was shut down and civilians truly had the freedom to move around the island.

This aerial photograph of Tanapag Harbor shows just how extensively the U.S. Navy built on Saipan, even as early as 1945. Courtesy of the U.S. Navy

Long after the war ended, however, civilians on Saipan still feared that their lives would be upended by another war that they had no part in starting. As Benigno Sablan states:

"The Japanese and U.S. fought the war, and we ended up paying the price for it."

Though the time after the war was not perfect, Saipan began to rebuild itself under the watchful gaze of the U.S. and United Nations. The relationship between the U.S. and Saipan strengthened, leading to the formation of the Commonwealth of the Northern Mariana Islands (CNMI) on 4 March 1976. This allowed for self-governing status under the umbrella of the federal government. Western ideals and values became part of everyday life on the island. Some islanders, like Gonzalo Pangelinan and his family, embraced the new government structure, claiming:

"We had a very good relationship with the Americans. And now, I'm proud to be an American."

The Swearing-In Ceremony for the first Commonwealth of the Northern Mariana Islands Legislature, Saipan 1978. Courtesy of Department of Public Affairs.

Others on the island have fought hard to keep their heritage alive in modern times. Lino Olopai reflects:

"After camp, life really changed. You have all this civil government, but I don't think that we knew what we were getting ourselves into. Carolinians have our traditions, and we have our elders that we would look upon for advice, assistance, and we have a chiefly clan that regulates the activity of the community or the island itself. And then you bring in a new government where you elect officials, your president, your mayor, your governor. It's totally different than our way, because we don't elect. Today, you have the freedom to choose, freedom of choice. You stand on your own two feet, be independent, don't depend on your parents, your friends. It's the western way of teaching, and it's totally different."

Conclusion

In the last few decades, archaeologists and historians have taken interest in studying all aspects of island life, spanning from pre-Colonial times to World War II. While the battle for Saipan has been heavily documented, much of the research and attention has been given to the U.S. and Japanese perspectives of war.

Slowly, the indigenous perspective has been moved to the forefront. The National Park Service has included a plaque next to Mount Carmel Cathedral regarding Camp Susupe, American Memorial Park now hosts a museum focused on the battle and subsequent internment, and the Marianas Memorial was erected, inscribed with the list of 933 indigenous civilians lost to battle and internment.

Younger populations have expressed interest in learning about what their family members have gone through during the battle for Saipan. Michael Camacho, son of David Camacho, recalls:

"I asked my dad about the war, because I was curious and I care about what he went through. He went through his mother dying, the war, then his brothers and dad passed away years later. It was overwhelming for me, but I never once saw him shed a tear. I'm amazed by him. My dad is my hero."

Many of the civilians that were interviewed for this project related that they shared their stories of battle and internment with their children and grandchildren. Felix Sasamoto shared his thoughts on the matter:

"I've passed on some short stories and memories to my children about hardships of the time, and I believe that the younger generation should know about it. Kids should know their own histories."

The Marianas Memorial in American Memorial Park.
Courtesy of the National Park Service

As a child, Isabel Villagomez remembers some aspects of the war, but not everything. She recalls:

"I was eight years old at the time of the war, born in 1936. In regards to the war, I was told to move away during story-telling between adults. My dad didn't feel that it was important to pass down the stories, and while I feel like they should be passed down, it's hard to do when I don't have the memories. "

As demonstrated in this compilation, there are many different stories and perceptions of the battle for Saipan and the internment of civilians. For a true narrative of war to be understood, it must include all stories and perspectives. In order for the indigenous civilian account of war to survive the test of time, stories must continue to be passed down to the younger generations.

REFERENCES

145th Field Artillery Battalion
1944 145th Field Artillery Battalion Journal, 1600 9 July- 1600 10 July 1944. National Archives, Washington, D.C.

Allen, Stewart D. and Judith R. Amesbury
2012 Commonwealth of the Northern Mariana Islands As a Fishing Community. U.S. Dep. Of Commerce, NOAA Technical Memorandum NMFS-PIFSC-36, Honolulu.

Amesbury, Judith R., Rosalind L. Hunter-Anderson, and Eleanor F. Wells
1989 Native Fishing Rights and Limited Entry in the CNMI. Micronesian Archaeological Research Services, Guam.

Bellas, Timothy H.
2011 The Trust Territory of the Pacific Islands (1947-1984). In The Northern Mariana Islands Judiciary: A Historical Overview, pp.35-42. Northern Mariana Judiciary Historical Society, Saipan.

Bellwood, Peter
2017 First Islanders: Prehistory and Human Migration in Island Southeast Asia. John Wiley & Sons, Hoboken.

Cabrera, Genevieve S.
2014 A Historical Overview of the Battle for Saipan. In Underwater Archaeology of a Pacific Battlefield: The WWII Battle for Saipan. J. Mckinnon & T. Carrell, editors. Springer Series in Archaeology, New York.

Camacho, Keith L.
2008 The Politics of Indigenous Collaboration. The Journal of Pacific History 43(2): 207-222.

2011 Cultures of Commemoration: The Politics of War, Memory, and History in the Mariana Islands. University of Hawai'i Press, Honolulu.

Castro, Marie S.C.
2014 Without a Penny in My Pocket: My Bittersweet Memories Before and After World War II. Dorrance Publishing, Pittsburgh.

Central Intelligence Agency (CIA)
2017 The Northern Mariana Islands. The World Factbook, Central Intelligence Agency <https://www.cia.gov/library/publications/the-world-factbook/geos/cq.html>. Accessed 12 March 2018.

Driver, Marjorie
1996 Carolinians in the Mariana Islands in the 1800s: Selected Documents from the Holdings of the Spanish Documents Collection at the Micronesian Area Research Center. Micronesian Area Research Center, Guam.

Dower, John W.
1993 War Without Mercy: Race and Power in the Pacific War. Pantheon Books, New York.

Duus, Peter
1996 Imperialism Without Colonies: The Vision of a Greater East Asia Co-prosperity Sphere. Diplomacy and Statecraft 7(1): 54-72.

Erskine, Brigadier General G.B.
1944 Annex DOG to Northern Troops and Landing Force Administrative Order Number 3-44 (FORAGER). Roll 1170, Reel A, Record Group 38, National Archives, College Park.

Falgout, Suzanne, Lin Poyer, and Laurence Marshall Carucci
2008   Memories of War: Micronesians in the Pacific War. University of Hawai'i Press, Honolulu.

Fold3
2018 Fold3 Online Database. Fold3 by Ancestry. https://www.fold3.com/. Accessed September 2017.

Fourth Marine Division
1944 Fourth Marine Division Operations Report- Saipan, Annex E: Special Comments. Roll 1256, Record Group 38, National Archives, Washington, DC. Accessed from Fold3 Digital Archives.

Goldberg, Harold J.
2007 D-Day in the Pacific: The Battle for Saipan. Indiana University Press, Bloomington.

Hezel, Francis X.
1988 From Conquest to Colonisation: Spain in the Mariana Islands 1690-1740. The Journal of Pacific History 23(2): 137-155.

1995 Strangers in Their Own Land: A Century of Colonial Rule in the Caroline and Marshall Islands. University of Hawaii Press, Honolulu.

Hughes, Matthew
2008 'Collateral Damage' and the Battle for Saipan, 1944. The RUSI Journal 153(6) 78-81.

Huie, William Bradford
1944 Can Do! The Story of the Seabees. Stratford Press, Inc., New York.

1945 From Omaha to Okinawa: The Story of the Seabees. Naval Institute Press, Annapolis.

Mac Lean, Lt. Commander Malcolm S.
1944 Fishing. Report on Observations of Civil Affairs Operations on Saipan, Tinian, and Guam. Northern Marianas Humanities Council, Digital Document Collections, U.S. Navy Civil Affairs Files (1944-1962). 1944, September.

Meller, Norman
1999 Saipan's Camp Susupe. Center for Pacific Island Studies, University of Hawai'i, Manoa.

McKinnon, Jennifer, Julie Mushynsky, and Genevieve Cabrera
2014 A Fluid Sea in the Mariana Islands: Community Archaeology and Mapping the Seascape of Saipan. Journal of Maritime Archaeology 9(1): 59-79

McMicken Collection
1945 Saipan State Historic Preservation Office Archives, McMicken Collection, 1945, Photo30.

Micronesian Area Research Center (MARC)
1981a The War Years on Saipan: Transcripts from Interviews with Residents Vol.1. Miscellaneous Publications No. 6, Micronesian Area Research Center.

1981b The War Years on Saipan: Transcripts from Interviews with Residents Vol.2. Miscellaneous Publications No. 6, Micronesian Area Research Center.

Morison, Samuel Elliot
1981 History of the United States Naval Operations in World War II: Vol. 8 New Guinea and the Marianas March 1944- August 1944. Little, Brown and Company, Boston.

Murray, Stephen C.
2006 War and Rememberance on Peleliu: Islander, Japanese, and American Memories of a Battle in the Pacific War. Ph.D Dissertation, University of California, Santa Barbara.

National Archives
1944 Saipan State Historic Preservation Office Archives, National Archives WWII Collection, 1944-1945, Photo 35.

2018 The National Archives Catalog. The U.S. National Archives and Records Administration. https://www.archives.gov/research/catalog. Accessed February 2017.

National Park Service
2018a Frequently Asked Questions: Results of Listing. National Register of Historic Places.
https://www.nps.gov/subjects/nationalregister/frequently-asked-questions.htm. Accessed 2 January 2019.

2018b Northern Mariana Islands. National Register of Historic Places. Digital Archive on NP Gallery. https://npgallery.nps.gov/NRHP/SearchResults/. Accessed 2 January 2019.

Naval History and Heritage Command
2017 World War II Cruise Books. U.S. Navy Seabee Museum. Naval History and Heritage Command.
https://www.history.navy.mil/content/history/museums/seabee/explore/wwii-cruisebooks.html. Accessed April 2017.

Northern Marianas Humanities Council
2018 Digital Document Collections. Northern Mariana Humanities Council. http://northernmarianashumanities.org/sec.asp?secID=21. Accessed April 2018.

Northern Troops and Landing Force
1944 Civil Affairs. Report Forager Phase I (Saipan), Section 4: Shore Part, Subsection N, Roll 1215, Record Group 38, National Archives, Washington, DC. Accessed from Fold3 Digital Archives.

NRHP- National Register of Historic Places
1980 Chalan Kanoa Historic District, Chalan Kanoa Japanese Structures, National Register of Historic Places Application. State Historic Preservation Office, Saipan.

Peattie, Mark R.
1998   Nan'yō: The Rise and Fall of the Japanese in Micronesia, 1885 - 1945. Pacific Islands Monograph Series 4. University of Hawaii Press, Honolulu.

Petty, Bruce M.
2002 Saipan: Oral Histories of the Pacific War. McFarland & Company Inc., Jefferson.

Richard, Dorothy E.
1957 United States Naval Administration of the Trust Territory of the Pacific Islands. 3 Volumes. U.S. Government Printing Office, Washington, D.C.

Russell, Scott
1998 Tiempon I Manmofo'na: Ancient Chamorro Culture and History of the Northern Mariana Islands. Micronesian Archaeological Survey, Division of Historic Preservation Report No. 32.

2017 From Company Town to Capital Village A Brief History of Chalan Kanoa, Saipan, CNMI. CNMI Division of Historic Preservation, Saipan.

Salaberria, Sister Maria Angelica
1994 A Time of Agony: The War in the Pacific in Saipan. Micronesia Area Research Center Educational Series, Guam.

Sasamoto, Felix
1950 Anatahan mission with Commander Johnson. Felix Sasamoto Personal Collection, Saipan.

Schmidt, Maj. Gen. Harry
1944 Report Covering Participation of Army Garrison Force, APO 244, in Marianas Operation, Section V-Civil Affairs Section G-5. Roll 1863, Record Group 38, National Archives, Washington, DC.

Spoehr, Alexander
2000 Saipan: The Ethnology of a War-Devastated Island, 2nd edition, Division of Historic Preservation.

Steward Collection
1944 Saipan State Historic Preservation Office Archives, Steward Collection, July 1944.

Townsend, Susan
2011 Japan's Quest for Empire 1931-1945. History: World Wars. BBC. http://www.bbc.co.uk/history/worldwars/wwtwo/japan_quest_empire_01.shtml

Tuten-Puckett, Katharyn (ed.)
2004 We Drank Our Tears: Memories of the Battles of Saipan and Tinian as Told By Our Elders. Pacific STAR Young Writers Foundation, Saipan.

Useem, Lt. John
1945 The American Pattern of Military Government in Micronesia. The American Journal of Sociology 51(2): 93-102.

1946 Social Reconstruction in Micronesia. Far Eastern Survey 15(1): 21-24.

United Nations
1945 Charter of the United Nations, Chapter XII International Trusteeship System, Article 76b. Accessed from http://legal.un.org/repertory/art76.shtml

United States Navy
1946 The Earthmover: A Chronicle of the 87th Seabee Battalion in World War II. World War Regimental Histories, 186.

2004 Camp Susupe: A Photographic Record of the Operation of Military Government on Saipan. Military Government Section Navy Number 3245. FPO San Francisco.

University of Hawaii
2019 Trust Territory of the Pacific Islands Photo Archives. Digital Archive Collections. UH Libraries, Univesity of Hawaii at Manoa. libweb.hawaii.edu/digicoll/ttp/ttpi.html. Accessed January 2019.

Yanaihara, Tadao
1940 Pacific Islands Under Japanese Mandate. Oxford University Press, London.

www.ingramcontent.com/pod-product-compliance
Lightning Source LLC
Chambersburg PA
CBHW041806160426
43202CB00001B/7